ISLAMIC LIFE

Firdos Tarannum

ISBN 978-93-5667-182-9
© Firdos Tarannum 2022
Published in India 2022 by Pencil

A brand of
One Point Six Technologies Pvt. Ltd.
123, Building J2, Shram Seva Premises,
Wadala Truck Terminal, Wadala (E)
Mumbai 400037, Maharashtra, INDIA
E connect@thepencilapp.com
W www.thepencilapp.com

Author biography

Firdos Tarannum is a teacher , with a degree in bachelor of science.She completed her school education in holy family school of Sindhanur, and completed her science field education in a renowned college called smj pu college, sindhanur.

Firdos Tarannum always admired of educating herself and others around her , she lived her life to the fullest before marriage and Alhamdulillah her every dream of educating the children completed.She taught some religious topics to the students of an islamic school where her parents studied which was a stepping stone of her teaching field, she completed the degree and started teaching in the same year immersing herself into two different roles everyday.She also gave tuition classes for the kids and also actively participated in courses of Islamic organisation held every week and ten days in summer months She also served as a science teacher in her own learned school for a year , which was a proud moment for her teacher seeing their student sitting with them on the same post at such an early stage.Lockdown throughout the world stopped the teaching of many teachers and one among them was firdos too.She completed her degree on the other hand successfully just before lockdown.During the times of lockdown she used them in a good way by handling around motivational or councilling sessions as her second dream is to help people with her words which have an immense effect on one's mind as people are often get themselves in depression and stress. She got married and gave birth to a wonderful son in a year of marriage itself Alhamdulillah. But this didn't stop her from completing her dreams. Tarannum is a housewife and a mother, who recently inspired herself to write the books after finding her love towards studies, she loved reading and was always appreciated for her work either for her teaching of 3 years or a councilling sessions.With her support of her spouse she now balances her work,child and book Her only dream is to, then to try have a weekend class for neighborhood children and often conduct workshop for dealing with mental health. At the same time , keeping herself educated and learn something everyday and teach something often so that this journey of her is continued by her children in sha Allah.If one loves something truly then it is the sole responsibility of oneself to take care of surroundings and their talent as well while fulfilling all their responsibilities

CONTENTS

Epigraph

In the name of Allah, the Entirely Merciful, the Especially Merciful.

[All] praise is [due] to Allah, Lord of the worlds – The Entirely Merciful, the Especially Merciful,

Sovereign of the Day of Recompense. It is You we worship and You we ask for help.

Guide us to the straight path –The path of those upon whom You have bestowed favor, not of those who have evoked [Your] anger or of those who are astray.

-AAMEEN

Introduction

Life is a roller coaster of emotions and every human experiences different emotions and reacts in a different way. Though how much one may neglect or reject but mental health plays a huge role in everyone's life. Sometimes the urge to express oneself leads to major disastrous decisions which leaves a mark of guilt throughout life. Everyone is fighting a different battle regardless of age, profession or experience, this should make us understand that religion has addressed this in the holy book several times that indeed trials are for humans and only a righteous believer will pass through it with patience and prayer .

Religion plays a crucial role in dealing with emotions but not everybody has a skill in dealing with it. Religion is not limited to festivals or rulings to be followed important moments of life like marriage, divorce, child birth, funerals, division of property...etc. sadly, our youth are getting away from religion because they think religion has nothing to do with the emotional balance of life although the emotions are at high level during the adulthood.

This book plays as a medium to connect our youth to religion because religion is not limited to the important aspects of life but it is important in every day's lives.

Being a Muslim one must have a basic knowledge of hadith, sunnah, life of our prophet peace be upon him. So, This book has also reminded the reader about some incidents of our Prophet's life so that the reader may realise that emotions were the same to every human regardless of atmosphere, time or age. The only boundary that needs to be crossed is to open up their mind that religion is not for your convenience it is indeed a guidance, a positive impact, a blessing and truly a right way which can be followed only by the one who really thinks to change himself.

The book also helps the reader to realise the emotions as normal by making the reader to express their emotions freely and the author has also tried her best to address the problems the youths are facing today from their homes to society. The core of the problems are deep but at the same time weak enough to break and change them .

The sole concentration of this book is to connect the reader to their religion to make them realise that our religion has given the equal importance to human emotions too, and at the same time it motivates the reader to open up and share their feelings and overcome their sadness by motivating themselves.

In the end, we as humans have no ability to change or to guide someone. It is only ALLAH who guides whom he wants.

So, we ask Allah to guide us to the straight path.

Aameen

BE GRATEFUL

Waking up from a comfortable bed, having a basic set of bathroom facilities with hot water, having a glass to drink fresh water, getting hot breakfast served on time everyday made by parents, good dress, healthy body...etc are a list of blessings which we think we deserve but actually we should be grateful for all those blessings but instead we behave arrogantly as if we did something great by living in this world to deserve, we often find ourselves finding faults with our blessings of our house being small, food being unhealthy, dress being not fashionable...etc.

our prophet peace be upon him was guaranteed the paradise yet, he cried in sujuud only because he wanted to thank Allah for his blessings . He didn't have food for days, enough clothes, lavish home,...etc yet his faith made him grateful.

You must be grateful for being a Muslim, being blessed with faith . All we can say is, the one who gave you blessings can also take them back in a fraction of a second because of your arrogance.

May Allah make us his grateful servants.

Aameen

DO NOT FORCE OTHERS

Forcing someone was never something you will notice as a recommendation in islam, if it was permissible then the first to force would have been our prophets, which could have been an easy way to spread Islam. But, it is and will never be an option to force somebody to change/act like you want or expect them to do.

Even our prophets had an option only to advise, and leave the rest upon Allah, but the concept of forcing is becoming common in every household like parents forcing their incompleted dreams to their kids, siblings forcing their younger ones to act like their order and at the end, the most famous ending quote will be "all we need is good for you ". But we fail to see that there is an another option like pray for their guidance which is Only in the hands of THE HAADI(THE GUIDER-Allah) , so it is important to realise that you can present your opinion, and pray for them and leave the rest upon Allah.

But never force anyone to be like you or act like you which can be done only by accepting the fact that not everyone is the same , infact your own kids are not of the same blood type. So you should realise that no one is going to change unless Allah wants, and the believer who feels the need to change himself.

May Allah guide us and change us

-Aameen

REFLECT AT YOUR FOOTSTEPS

Our prophet peace be upon him accepted himself the way he was, soft hearted like the petals of rose, his smile lwas ike a flower blooming ,his walk was like a man of strength and courage and eyes filled with haya and eemaan. There was a point when he was sad when no one believed him, no one accepted him, many of them betrayed him, he lost his sons, wife and many of his companions yet he didn't question himself nor Allah.

while Today at even for small problems we question our lord and blame him for all our difficulties. we should Look what has happened to our lives today, we complain and compare our lives to everybody surrounding us, we want a car like we see on social media, we want to do vlogs and share our lives with 1000 others whom we don't know, we now want to eat every delicious food and visit every rich place, we want haram relationships, we want to enjoy our lives like it has no end, what has our lives become, what is the value of your life in your eyes?

We cannot complain and blame the society for our sins because even our prophet was surrounded by same sins like shirk ,alcohol ,adultery---etc. but never did he complain because he was being himself and he was guided by Allah as he was on the right way. on the other hand today people do all the negative activities and expect positive result , look what have they done to themselves ‹ They are

on a road of destruction , whose consequences will be beared by their kids and many more generations- it is high time to understand that life is unpredictable , within a moment everybody can be under the soil-
let the fear of meeting Allah enter our heart , let the body shiver before committing sins by imagining the punishment of hereafter, let the foots shake and tremble as they can't run away from death. so pause, reflect at the way we are going, change the route if the end of it is hellfire.

May Allah guide us to the straight path

Aameen

PRAYER OF COUPLE

We see commonly that after the marriage the couple pray together for the first time and it ends there, but this should be a daily habit. Because it has an unimaginable impact on a relationship of a couple.

let the day of couple start with a prayer where the husband leads and the wife follows, this creates the leadership quality among the husband to lead his family and the wife to accept him as the head of her family and creates a positive energy to start the day with. Let the tahajjud be a strong means of bond between the couple, where they pray and read Qur'an together, As the day begins eventually both of them may get busy with their duties but praying together should be a practice between a family Because it is an important foundation of love between the creator and the creations.

All this seems and looks beautiful as you are in the early phase of marriage as the duo has very much attraction towards each other and they try to understand each other and compromise out of love. But after a few months, all this changes and that is not in a negative way but that is how a life goes with some changes, but the habit of praying together once atleast in a day should be important Because during early days it may seem no impact Because of excess love all around but as the time passes, the duo surely face some tests or difficulties in any form like wealth, health, child, relationship, understanding....etc . All this chaos results into disaster when the couple verbally exchange words out of anger and all of a sudden the love may seem fading away but remember whenever this happens let not this anger stop you from praying together like everyday, it may seem difficult or impossible to stand and look at each other yet pray pray and pray for the sake of Allah.

The satan enjoys the fight of couple and leaves no stone unturned to increase the distance between them . The couple must realise that prayer is important not only to make tem strong but also to compromise and accept each other. The distance can be reduced only with the love of prayer that gets strong with each word of quran recitation because the matter will be handled by the creator who increases the love between them.

The real effect of prayer is seen when you obey Allah first instead of each other, then a sign of peace, tranquility and calmness surround you when you start praying and till the end of the prayer, all negativity vanishes making a way for love again. After the prayer all you feel is a minute of silence among each other which was impossible just before the prayer but once after the prayer you will have a calm mind to accept the faults of each other, respect each other and to apologise and move on. That is the power of prayer which energizes you to live again and try again and understand again and to compromise a little more again but this time not for eachother but only for Allah.

May Allah bless all the couples to pray together, stay together in duniya and hereafter.

Aameen

DO NOT BE A RUMOUR CARRIER

Carrying a rumour is a trend followed by everyone these days intentionally or unintentionally. Rumours are thought to be initially a form of time pass but it ends with some of the certificates of character given by rumour carriers.

Even our prophet peace be upon him was a target of it, there were many rumours about him labelling him as the magician, poet... etc which is clearly mentioned in the Qur'an. Even when the prophet knew about these rumours he could have clearly given an explanation about it ,but he chose to remain silent because rumours are of no value.

How often do we make a judgement about a person even before meeting them, like a person is strict, clingy, bossy, arrogant...etc and somehow these labels make up our mind regarding others and we often end up treating them the way they don't deserve.

Just think what if someone treated you badly because they already heard a rumour about you which was not true, your side of story was never heard.

These rumours often kill a person internally because these affect them hard. rumours are not only about physical appearance, they are usually of character, attitude, body, status, family and exposing someone's sins too.

what can you do to avoid the rumours as they reach us unannounced most of the time,
So beware when you hear about others,
Ignore them
 Do not judge others based on what you heard, we are no one to judge . As the reality is always Different from what you heard
Stop the rumour carrier by cross questioning
Leave if the matter is not related to you
Do not carry on the rumour just to get clarification.

May Allah save us from becoming a rumor carrier.

Aameen

OPINIONS ARE EVERYWHERE

Everybody has their own opinion, that needs to be respected, as our prophet peace be upon him did so. He had a role to Express the religion in the best possible way and did not force it to others to accept but the non believers who could have accepted or rejected it chose to be violent by harming other believers physically and thereby leading themselves to hell.

Everybody has a choice like our religion has given, guidance is for everyone but not everybody accepts it hence, we decide our fate in the hereafter by our own choice and opinions.

The society is full of opinionated people ‹ but often people fail to realise when to express them.

let a mother decide how to take care of her child, let a father decide for the future of his family, let a child decide what to be his goal. even if they make 99 mistakes for the 100th time they will learn on their own but we see people who forcefully express their opinion Because they did so in a role at a time where others are now and thereby criticise them for not accepting it‹ And at the end they choose to harm them verbally or mentally. So, remember that everybody has an opinion that needs to be respected and only the wise ones know when and where to express it .Your opinion has a great value, do not lose it's worth by expressing it everywhere.

This should not let you think that you should not accept any opinion but be wise enough to differentiate which opinion is useful for you or may help you. do not accept every opinion and get depressed by knowing, rather have a clear mind and realise who your well wishers are.

May Allah help us to accept and respect others opinion.

Aameen

PRAYER IS LOVE

After a certain time of marriage, the family completes with the children but the couple fail to introduce prayer to the children.

Since , at a very young age prayer is recommended in islam but is made compulsory after the age of seven, because Islam knows the value of prayer, but what we see is, parents introducing the prayer as a force or a fear of fire like "pray or else Allah will burn you, beat you .etc" this creates a mindset of negative image of the creator. So the child reads prayer for the sake of parents, with the fear of being asked about it later and we see kids stop praying, if they see their friends not praying or when they see their own parents leaving the prayer because of worldly activities like functions, marriages, outing, meeting etc it Creates a mindset that prayer is only important when you have time and they feel it as ok to miss a prayer, which makes the kid to stop praying after attaining puberty that "am going to hell atlast why is the need to pray, am healthy why should I pray, let me repent at my old age like my parents" eventually these feelings is nowadays taking our youth away from prayer.

NOTE FOR PARENTS TO BE-
When you get to know about pregnancy, read Qur'an regularly,(note that there is no particular surah like Maryam

and yusuf to read during pregnancy) by heart lots of supplications ..etc . Let one of any parent accept it as a duty to recite Qur'an infront of kids daily.

AFTER BECOMING PARENTS-

Introduce prayer as a fun to your kid (toddler), let them read book, let them tear, let them know what Quran is, introduce them to know the letters of quran like you teach them communication, there is no specific time to teach them about religion. let them learn daily at any time or everytime, take your kid to pray with you , put a small prayer mat beside you, put some books, tazbeeh around , let them see what and how you pray. You will see without you making an effort child learns sujuud, ruku, rakah, salam , dua, wadhu ..etc

All these acts needs no effort just be you.

After a certain time when kid starts walking let the father take them to masjid on weekend, let them play there , buy some chocolates upon return this creates curiosity for them to go to the masjid , let them make friends in masjid let them see what masjid is, what happens there, what he should do, what is his father doing...

Let him go on a weekend kids lectures of islam happening in your neighborhood..etc

Let him share with his mother what he did, let the mother advise what he should do next time,..etc

These all acts needs no effort, your kid notices what you do daily, not what you make them to learn at specific time

Parents should not have a goal for their children instead parents should work on their eeman and the environment to be happy and cheerful. so that the kid learns that religion needs no specific time to practice in life, instead our life should be around religion in sha Allah.

If you pray your kids will pray without you asking for it.

If you neglect, they will too and it is the biggest loss a parent can have in this duniya and hereafter. As it's loss may not appear right away but will eventually appear when the parent finds no way for the negligence they did with the religion. The loss may be temporary in this world but in the hereafter the punishment will be severe and permanent so, be strict with your religious responsibilities for indeed your laziness may destroy a generation.

May Allah bless our parents, children and family and strengthen us to create an environment of righteousness around.

Aameen

WORDS HAVE POWER TO HEAL

The whole biography of Our prophet peace be upon him is an evidence, not a single person, complained about the rude words of our prophet. Even his own servant is a witness of our Prophet's kind words. What are we doing today? Let us just check ourselves,

How rude are we to our siblings, servants, parents, friends...etc. not a single sentence is completed without using abusive words . these are not from Islam.

Remember, if someone was unkind to us we curse them throughout our life, what are we doing in return. it's high time to Stop the blame game, we cannot blame the world always to be cruel because eventually we are also a part of it.

So, be kind with your words , we are extremely kind with the guests and extremely rude to our own family, this is not islam. Although these are the people who deserves more love , but we treat each other like they are our paid servants or sinners. This is not Islam.

We keep Posting good thoughts on social media while on the other side your own loved ones are a victim your unkind words. This is not Islam.

Please understand that whatever you say from your mouth needs to be corrected or think twice before speaking because.what you said cannot be taken back and sometimes either sorry may not heal them or it is too late to correct your words. Think and understand before it's too late.

May Allah make us kind towards each other

Aameen

CORRECTING OTHERS

Our prophet peace be upon him, corrected others but not always because the more he tried to correct others by inviting them towards Islam, the more people were turning violent. So Allah allowed him to do his best , but he also said it is Allah's duty to guide his servants.

We see everywhere today people correcting others in the comment section of social media,stories in our posts, in our houses parents correcting their child at their every step, teachers getting strict with everything, siblings correcting younger ones in everything...etc

Do not take the burden of changing everything and everyone around you. let your shoulders have some rest. Change your thinking first by lightening the burden of changing the world. You cannot do so, everybody knows what they have to do , no one is dumb , they will bear the consequences on their own if they were wrong in their decision . But, we go on wasting time on others.

Hold on a second, look at yourself, do you really think there is nothing wrong with you or you are really perfect..? NO! We are not .

It is not an advise to stop correcting others but just an opinion that, There is a time to correct others but only till an extent , do not push others that they start to avoid you. Do not annoy others , and then we complain of others about ignoring us, this is the response of your own actions

. We insult, humiliate, crack jokes and what not in order to correct them. Who are you to correct others.. correct yourself before others. Pray for them before correcting. Your respect is in your hands .

Unfortunately society is full of overly educated people who wants to correct everything like what others should wear, eat, sleep, look like ..etc. Thus, we lose our respect in the eyes of our own family because of over-commenting and over interference and overly correcting others at every step. The more you correct others forcefully everyday and every minute the more you lose your respect.

May Allah help us to correct ourselves before correcting others.

Aameen

CHANGE YOURSELF FIRST

*"Changing yourself is easier than changing others"*would sound better. As we try harder to change others , on the other hand changing ourselves would be a lot easier.

This only means that changing others would bring less benefit to you while if you change yourself would have a greater benefit in your character.

Our prophet peace be upon him led a life full of changes, our prophet had the most unique way to change others what was that?

HE FOLLOWED THE RELIGION FIRST,

thereby proving a point that the religion is actually more easier to follow by actually showing it practically.

We order others to pray correctly, don't watch filth or movies, don't listen to music..etc. but others may have never witnessed you doing all of these.

How often parenting fails because our own parents fail to bring religion into their own character and home, thereby a generation fails to bring up the religion. Change yourself first before trying to change others because we order, we force, we explain others with a detailed hadith and authentic sources but we fail to change ourselves, to change our prayer by slowing it a little more, we fail to read Qur'an a little more, we fail to give charity, we fail to do some more extra deeds.How we often fail to do something extra for our religion and change something within ourselves first, we go on blaming others for their sins and boast our good deeds and we are the ones who commit sins privately.

What has happened to us, why do we blame each other and curse each other for the sins, we stop others from filth while our inner side is full of filth. We hold a banner of judgement to change others all day while at night we commit grave sins.

This doesn't mean you should not help others to change, it only means "you should concentrate more, atleast 90% of your concentration should be on changing yourself for good".

Realise, your character needs to change not outward but inward because that is how the judgement will be, nothing will benefit if your inner character is worst . Because what you are inside, will be the result of your place on the judgement day.

May Allah help us to change ourselves first.

Aameen

REPENT BEFORE DEATH

Two youngsters lost their lives in an accident, a family man with three daughters with the youngest of only two months died during a rainstorm and one of our elders died a while ago. A newly married couple of only two months dies by the electric device blast, what were there plans for future, just when they thought of a life full of happiness , everything came to end within a blink of an eye. These cases made me realise everyone had repentance lined up for a certain time, youngsters were about to repent in their old life, but who guaranteed you that you will be alive?

All these cases should be a lesson for us to repent but we all are busy scrolling on the phone, pushing away the accounts which says about religion, following the accounts who post songs, following every Trend, chatting, mixed gatherings, lazy to pray, but always ready to go out with friends, hating those who say good, opening Qur'an only when someone forces you or it is Ramadan, sleeping during Fajr and waking up all night watching all the filth, reading and running away from prayer in a speed, rushing for prayer with an incomplete wadu, ending the prayer without dhikr, spending the day without astagfaar... etc. Who has guaranteed you that you have enough time to repent.

This world is only around you for a moment that will end with a status and story of your photo with a caption of

MISS YOU MY BRO..and that is all , how they are gonna end your identity.

Think, think what are you running for and from whom are you running, the world, the cars, the houses, the vacation , the degree,...etc. Remember, your friends not even your parents...no one would enter with you in the grave.

Do not think this trap to be that easy to end one moment and in just a second you will be under the soil. And your time of judgement begins.

Help yourself today to wake up from the bed, open the Qur'an, read, make good company. In the end, you are and will be alone. Do not run because this is the reality.. repent before it's too late.

May Allah accept our repentance before our death.

Aameen

WOMAN - HOME MAKER OR WRECKER

The difference in the atmosphere of the house is not only because of it's surroundings it's mostly because of the woman who runs the house. Though the man takes the decision but it is the woman who follows the decision.

You can easily notice, the woman who keeps the religion as base for her family may feel difficult to raise up her children in the righteous way but eventually at the end she will give rise to those children who will lead her to the Jannah even after her death, and value her the most till the time she is alive. The woman who wakes up her children to pray, who narrates the story of prophets, who reads the Qur'an with her children, whose house is always filled with recitation of the Qur'an, who forbids filth(movies/songs) in her home, who guides her young children to abide by hijab and lower their gaze, who leads the home all in the way of religion will never fail. This is the woman who makes her home

But, today we see women who love to lead only themselves in their passion, don't want to marry, and never want to have children because of their responsibility , even after having children they hand them to some caretaker, openly sins and allows kids to do so. You can see today women allowing their young kids to go for mixed

Gatherings with make up on, encouraging their children to dance on the music, follow every trend, their kids never accept hijab because their own mother never hide her beauty, they see their mother talking openly to non mehrams without hijab, openly watches filth with kids, curses/abuses often, their kids don't pray or read Qur'an because their mother never did so, this is the woman who wrecks her own Home. The woman who cries in this world and hereafter too because she failed herself and her family and thereby faces a great loss because her children doesn't value her in this world and forget her existence right after her burial.

This all begins with just a decision of marriage where a woman is brought into the responsibility of husband, the way the man leads the home and the way the woman leads are different because even if the man has religious knowledge, he cannot teach everything to his kids and even if he orders the wife to teach the kids she can't do so because she cannot give what she doesn't know. so, it is important for a woman more than a man to have religious knowledge. so, choose wisely for indeed it is the responsibity of a woman to lead and feed her children.

This is why our religion always asked our youngsters to marry the righteous one because the woman may raise a generation but in what way depends upon the faith of the woman. The woman may either make or destroy a generation.

May Allah bless us with a spouse who is righteous.

Aameen

REMINDING FAVOURS

Our prophet peace be upon him And his companions were a helping source for each other, in every matter of living, safety, food, war and religion. What kept the love strong was the person who helped never reminded them nor the one who accepted help never remained ungrateful.

You can see We are growing now in such a time that everyone around us reminds each other of the favour done by them, as if they have a loan to get repayed. And When someone fails to help , they are the first one to remind you "i did this/that for you, i took so much pain for you, i struggled for you, i gave birth to you, cooked for you, looked after you, you are an irresponsible man , it's time to repay the favour, i helped you with money, business, home....etc" all these may seem pretty normal in every aspect but the one who hears it feels the pain. It is almost very common that the parents are expecting the favours to get repayed in the form of obedience from their own children, as if raising them was not their duty but a favour that they always expected to get returned in their old age.

But, The reality is no one has asked you to help, it was you who felt pity to help others, no one has asked you to give birth it was your choice to raise them in a certain manner, so, blaming others of ungratefulness is not a good thing. Help with an intention of gaining a reward in the hereafter but most people's real intention is often expressed by constant reminding. This is the least level to which a human can go to hurt others. The human loses everything the self respect in this World and the reward in the hereafter too.

 What makes you a human is to help others but the thing that makes you a good human is to remain silent when you have all the chances of reminding the favours yet you remain silent for the sake of Allah. Whatever you do even if it is to speak something good let that be for the sake of Allah, the moment you do something good forget it for the sake of Allah, if the moment arrives to get your favour returned, never remind for the sake of Allah. Feel grateful that Allah has made you capable enough to help others.

May Allah help us to help others but never remind them.

Aameen

THE WAY YOU SPEAK

Our prophet peace be upon him always brought out the special talents of his companions like Bilal radhi allahu anhu for his mesmerizing voice, Umar radhi allahu anhu for his fighting skills..etc he always admired others even behind their backs he defended them.But we see people around us today often complaining or speaking bad about others.

Remember whatever someone says about others is a certificate of their own character.

Parents insulting relatives, guests, siblings Insulting each other behind their backs, friends insulting each other ...etc are proof of how we are raised . While there are still some people who always make dua for each other even behind their back, these people are worth to be appreciated.

Remember, the people who criticize others behind their backs also criticise you without letting you know, try your best to avoid those people who have a habit of backbiting, sadly our family members also enjoy these sins , so when you notice that the topic is going out of context get outside and do not enter till they change the topic. Do not even nod as yes for backbiting nor go deep into the conversation by enquiring about it, leave the place as soon as you can. Because, **saving your faith is lot more important than saving your relationship with those who enjoy sins.**

May Allah make us among those who pray for each other.

Aameen

PERCEPTIONS

Life is full of perceptions, at every stage of life we have perceptions like we have perceptions of a good college, good studies, parents having a perception that only their kids are good, kids having the opposite perception about parents , partners having perceptions about each other...etc. all these perceptions take a worst turn often making us feel depressed because our perceptions doesn't meet the reality.

 if the perception was good and the reality was bad it effects us badly and thereby breaking our heart

 If our perceptions about our loved ones was they would serve us, obey us and if they don't do so , we turn opposite and start being rude . Who asked you in the first place to consider a perception about others and they didn't know it and you all of a sudden expect them to follow your perception.

 Society is turning their own perceptions into reality, if something is missed from a place our direct doubts go on our servants, if your child attracts a bad habit we think his friends made him do this... these perceptions are breaking the society and a kind of creating a generation where everyone is trying to turn their own perceptions into reality.

Remember, have a perception about yourself first and let that be always a good perception, try your best to turn them into a reality.

Never have a perception about others, because one or the other day when you meet reality, you will get hurt.

As it's a human nature to think always good about himself and bad about others.

may Allah help us to think good about each other

aameen

STAND FOR YOURSELF

Standing up for yourself and self respect is a term in society which is always claimed as not a part of good character.

Our prophet peace be upon him stood for himself and religion often. There are also some incidents where he remained silent because the person was not approachable. Today, society gives the same advice or expects from every younger one to remain silent when the elders are talking either the words are hurting or insulting or humiliating doesn't matter, sometimes the words or the actions are also not permissible in Islam yet the younger ones are always forced to stay silent and when they complain they are often made to hear BE PATIENT. Well, the other side of the story is to look upon the one who is saying wrong, irrespective of the role or relationship one needs to check the fact that primarily what was said was permissible or not, is it worth hearing or not, were the words kind or not. This doesn't mean the younger ones should always raise their voice to every petty thing but this also doesn't give the right to elders to say or do whatever they want and then justify it by saying am the elder, you need to respect me though however you disrespect me .. etc. Elders today seems to have the remote to control over everything of their younger ones, they don't trust them with anything, they like to decide everything on their behalf, they term them as incapable to face the problems of life and this they attach themselves to their life to protect them and save them . In all these circumstances, the younger ones raise themselves with only thinking that they need someone to guide them in person for their whole life, they feel under confident, they think that whatever the elders say/order is right for them but

The book of guidance has clearly guided that the people who follow their forefathers blindly, have no brains of their own, because they don't think anything. So,

Have courage to stand up for yourself without disrespecting.

Standing up for yourself is not a sign of disrespect, rather it is a sign of your self confidence.

Not every wrong thing is acceptable just because your loved ones are doing it.

The elders should also understand the opinions of younger ones and give them the freedom to taste the difficulties of life and guide them instead of forcing the decisions. The elders should not think the younger ones as incapable of living life on their own.

With time everything changes and the thinking should also change and accept the fact of this world without bragging their generational decisions on their younger ones especially when there is a huge gap of time between the two generations.

May Allah help us to stand up for ourselves.

Aameen ❣

EVIL SPREADS FAST

Evil spreads faster mostly because of the people who let it happen, they decide to save themselves first rather than the society and they choose to run back from the place rather than standing up to defend it with courage, they are the coward people whose tongue and hands are weak besides being healthy.

When you stand silent when evil is taking place one or the other may happen.

.if you are a good person you will have a regret that why did the evil happen and why didnt you stood against it thus thereby you will for sure try to stand against it next time and if you are a bad person then the evil will have a no impact on you. Because It takes a lot of courage to talk back and stand straight against the wrong. It costs nothing when there are unknown people opposite to you but when you are standing opposite to your loved ones you lose more than gaining, like losing love, trust etc those people expect you to accept every right or wrong they do. But as soon as you stand opposite all you get is negative vibes and negativity all around, all of a sudden everything seems so different you feel that you did wrong but wait ..

Remind yourself when you stood opposite to your loved ones you stood for one strong creator that is Allah, and he knows everything, wait a little while, fight a little more , the more it is hard to bear the more near is your victory.

It may take years for your loved ones to understand why you opposed them, they may also warn you off cutting the relationship but what should make you get going is you are strengthening your relationship with Allah. Everyone will leave you alone but the relationship with Allah continues after this world too, And you should stop constantly explaining to others why you opposed them in order to get sympathy or concern , because Allah knows your intentions. Because even after your explanation they blame you for satisfaction and criticize and shame you infront of others. Let not your voice shake or fall weak when you are speaking for the right thing.Be strong be steadfast be more patient.

May Allah help us to stand straight against the wrong

Aameen

ACCEPT YOUR PARENTS

Our parents often try to give all of those facilities to you which once they admired to have. Right from the moment of your birth , there is not even a single thing which they haven't sacrificed for you, sleeplessness, money, time, health, hard work and sometimes desires they sacrifice everything to give you the best .

When we lived with our parents in our childhood all we wanted was the partnership with our parents, we expected them to be with us everywhere. But, As we grow and join the society we change our mindset and till we reach the teenage years, we get embarrassed by everything they do.

The parents who made us learn talking, walking and clothing. We are today embarrassed by every single thing of them once they taught us. We no longer want them to be with us in our school or college functions, we avoid going with them to the gatherings of our lifestyle, we no longer want to ask them anything because we think they always respond negatively.

Remember, if it was the case then Allah would never have given them the authority of YOUR JANNAH in their hands. You agree to it or not but, every parent goes through a lot to bring up their kids in their best way. Do not be embarrassed to be with them, to go with them, to ask them about their health and basic facilities, to take care of them. All of this needs only a little pateince and silence to deal with. Because once they are lost you lose the precious chance of gaining the Jannah as no matter how much you hurt them they will never hurt you back and instead they are the first ones to forgive you.

May Allah bless all our parents and make us their righteous children.

Aameen

GIFT OTHERS

Gifting others is for sure something worth a good deed.

A special kind of satisfaction and peace is felt in the heart when you gift others, remember no matter the size of the gift value should be the giver of the gift . The best gift would be the Qur'an eventually the greatest source of sawaabe jaariya .

We often see people accepting gifts with their hands and rejecting it through the heart and often complaining about it, resulting in the reciever of the gift trying to give the same type or price of gift when he thinks to gift them in return.

Whatever you recieve gift large or small when you are turn arrives to gift something, try your best to give it for the sake of Allah, gift without expecting anything in return, gifting others will always give you satisfaction, never shame or criticise the gift you receive.

May Allah help us to gift others often with a good intention.

Aameen

SIGN OF RIGHTEOUSNESS

Feeling restless or uneasiness is often good especially when there is something very bad or sinful activities taking place, people may judge you for acting weird but be thankful that atleast your heart is alive to feel the wrong going on, an urge to stop or change the place may seem impossible and you may reach to an extent that you cannot explain nor stay in a place because the more you stay the more energy of your positivity will drain you and take you to an extent that sins seems you normal and good deeds feels difficult to do. Do not reach to this extent that a sinful place doesn't create fear in your heart and you have no impact about the place you are living in. Be careful because what you see and where you live is the result of the character you carry or the attitude you accept. Our prophet peace be upon him often loved to live alone to deeply feel the urge towards going right because he knew what sins were going around him and Thus he usually went in a cave for some time to understand his heart.prophet Noah was advised to leave the place because no matter how much he did the people never changed, so he left the place without his son. Even Allah knew that the disbelievers were not going to change and it would hurt our prophet more so, Allah asked him to leave the place and start our religion in a new atmosphere.Sometimes you have to leave the place not because you love yourself only because you tried everything to change but it is better to leave the place alone for the right thing then to go with the wrong.

The first thing to change something is to realise the wrong happening and the urge to change because if you feel wrong as right then you also feel the person as wrong who teaches you right . Do not lose hope and be thankful for feeling restless in a negative atmosphere, try to advise and change if nothing works then shift yourself because you will die alone and you will be asked only about your deeds so save yourself, do not sail on the boat of haram because the sailor is your loved one. Choose wisely because Allah has blessed you with an understanding of right and wrong.

May Allah help us to save ourselves from this wordly fitna.

Aameen

PRAY, SUPPLICATION AND HOPE

These are the three simple words to say and hear but when it comes to follow it is the most difficult thing to accept. We pray as if it's a matter of seconds, supplicate as if we don't need anything and we lose hope often because we think we don't deserve mercy . All these are the Whispers of Satan and degrade your faith steadily, these actions if not applied correctly will have no impact on your personality.

Pray , pray and pray with a purpose. Our prayer gets longer only when the hardships or trials becomes harder this is the way we treat the prayer as if it is important to pray only during difficulties.

Supplicating without following the etiquettes and ending it faster as it's just a full stop of our prayer.

And we hope to get forgiven for every major and minor sin while we don't leave the sin nor do we do any good deeds yet we hope for Jannah at the highest level with the sins of the cheapest level.

Our prophet peace be upon him prayed often either for others , during difficulties, when he felt sad or depressed, when he was happy, he asked, repented, acted gratefully, thanked Allah for the blessings, asked Allah to save him from the torment of the grave, questions of judgement and he also prayed for his ummah.

Follow our prophet, pray as if it is last and **supplicate each time**with different words and purpose , **never lose hope nor during happiness and sadness.**
 have hope that you will be forgiven, so repent often and constantly.

May Allah accept our prayers and supplications.

Aameen

CRACKING A CHILD'S SOUL

We all remember an incident where we witnessed our parents fighting, but if it was once or twice throughout your life it is fine. Because parents try hard not to fight and they regret that moment too where the child was affected due to their fight.

But if you have grown up witnessing your parents fight often and regularly then it effects the child's mental health. you will witness some major effects as the child grows and till he reaches the adult stage he accepts getting angry, frustrated, hitting objects and people as a part of his own personality. He may not express it often but it slowly becomes his own personality. The people are no longer interested in communicating with him and thus he slips into depression. Or the other effect is the child loses his own personality, ability, talent,...etc and thus becomes an introvert because whole life he loves to escape like he has grown up escaping the fight of his own parents.

In any case the child loses his own identity and accepts himself which he is not.

The main effect of the child's personality is beared by his own parents, they complain about him to the society being disobedient and unfaithful, not serving, dutiful and respecting them . The question should be asked to the parents first that what duty did they complete when they gave him birth, the child comes into the world with some duty of being asked and understood and fulfills his basic rights. The right also includes teaching, introducing, guiding, helping him follow the religion...did the parents do that? The right to serve him into the religion is more important than serving him the basic needs. Otherwise you fail to distinguish yourself from animals because animals also give birth , provide food and leave them. Today, parents are giving birth, appointing an assistant and turning their back from their own kids . If you haven't showed them why you deserved Jannah or why was the key and door of Jannah assigned to you as parents then how can you expect him to serve you to enter the Jannah which he thinks you are not capable of .. Auuzubillah. It is a story of every house today that parents ignore their child and the child ignores them later. What you sow, you shall reap.

Our prophet peace be upon him loved the kids and other kids too . He loved to watch the kids play, how nicely he introduced the kids to pray by taking them on his shoulder .. etc .

But parents today find the religion as a good reason to hit their own children as they can't beat their spouse during an argument, so they find comfort in their evil soul by hitting the children. You are cracking his soul O parent! **The body scars may heal but the scar of his heart remains fresh till his death.**You are cracking his identity, personality, character, attitude and soul.

Understand before it's too late for you to regret. For you may die soon in this world before bearing the consequences of your evil acts but there is a permanent punishment in the hereafter. Fear Allah,for indeed Allah is just .

May Allah protect the child from mental trauma.

Aameen

LIST YOUR BLESSINGS

The best thing about islam is we start our day with the prayer, a communication which is special only between you and your creator. No one knows what you have talked about, and the best part is your creator knows even the unsaid words . The day is the laziest one where you missed our Fajr prayer and the most active day is the day where you prayed Fajr and tahajjud too.

Our lord has ordered us to pray Fajr and read the Qur'an after that and he let us to feel the advantages of it. Today scientists are listing out the advantages of waking up early and reading and unknowingly we have been doing it for years.

Even our supplication and prayer starts with the praising of our lord, this shows the impact of starting everyday with positivity.

A little more positivity is noticed in the character of the person who is grateful to his lord.

TASK - As soon as your day begins or ends make a list of 5-10 different blessings everyday.

This makes you

More grateful towards your lord.

Less complainer and arrogant.

A content believer.

A faithful and obedient servant.

When you feel there is a lack of motivation to survive or

lack of faith then read the blessings aloud which is enough to make you feel that atleast you have these things to survive.

May Allah make us his grateful servants.

Aameen

EXPRESS YOUR PAIN

Words fall short when pain endures longer, every person in a state of life goes through the pain, where he wants to say something but nobody wants to understand, when he wants to grow but nobody cares, when he wants to cry but nobody has the shoulder to lend you help, when you want to say but nobody has the time to hear. But remember prophet peace be upon him also went through a state where nobody cared about the pain he went through but it was Allah who helped him , cared and supported him. Remember the one who gave birth to you fails to value you because they are the creations of Allah they are humans with defaults and they have their own life. Depending on Allah Because he created you, he knows even before you express, he knows even before you say , the one with whose permission the leaf falls also grants the permission for your eyes to let your tears fall.

Only guarantee as a believer i can give you is if your painful tears fall in sujuud near Allah he will for sure never let you cry in front of others, he will protect you because you asked for it by crying, he will help you even if you didn't ask for it. You don't need anyone if Allah is with you You don't need the soothing words of anyone when Allah has revealed the whole Qur'an for you.

You don't need to owe any explanations to anyone when Allah knows your intentions.

You don't need to put a step backward when you go forward for the sake of Allah.
You don't need to change your decision when you decide for the sake of Allah.
Only condition is **do everything for the sake of Allah.**

Allah knows best

ADVISE WITHOUT HUMILIATING

How often do we notice that humiliating is often misunderstood as Advising while this may create a chaos of negative feelings in the heart of listener. Like when we correct our elders we get a negative response like *"ohhh now you will advise us/ what have you seen in life to advise us/ the egg whose shell is not broken yet will now teach us/ what is your experience of life to guide us / do you really think you are elder to us now / we know more than you/ shut up / do not interfere we are not interested in your advise...etc"*although your advise may come in a respectful way without any humiliation but our society has set some boundaries that younger ones are not eligible to advise elder ones , younger ones always need the advise or they are not capable of living on their own...etc. and thus when our own children advise us we get a negative response and elders expect from younger to always obey every advise they give .

How often do we try to advise and when in return we don't get any response or get humiliated. We stop advising them because it affects us , we start to feel bad and we are made to feel worthless to say anything. We are often targeted as a form of humiliation but remember our prophet peace be upon him was humiliated physically and mentally for the right advice this didn't stop him from advising. So advise people but do not humiliate while doing so because you will lose your own worth and respect if you question others dignity and respect while advising.

May Allah prevent us from humiliating others.

Aameen

TIME CHANGES EVERYTHING

How often do we think time is taking longer to pass during difficulties and time flew faster than wind during happiness, but in reality time doesn't change speed. What changes is your emotions and everybody wants happiness to stay and difficulties to pass. How many times do we think that it is impossible for us to face life and we decide to end life but having a little patience and hope corrects everything and we act thankfully that we survived. What almost seems impossible, gets possible only with a little patience and hope. Remember our religion also spreads with the patience and hope of a single person that is our prophet peace be upon him and today every city has tens to thousands of muslims. Though to spread well takes time but it is not impossible. Just don't lose hope, be courageous to walk on the right path, know that Allah is with the right ones, there is no obedience to anyone not even your own desires to the disobedience of Allah, have faith that everything will be alright, you may get negative thoughts in fact suicidal and depressed thoughts fight them for the sake of Allah, every change takes time to accept and your difficulties will also be turned into blessings one day in sha Allah, do not turn back after fighting for the right thing only because the wrong ones are stronger than you , do not stop fighting just because you are tired, try once again with a little more hope and patience, it may take time but eventually it will pass, be strong.

May Allah heal whatever is hurting you.

Aameen

SUPPLICATE TO CHANGE

We do everything to complete the task but we fail to make an attempt near our lord, how often did a problem take so long to get solved but as soon as we pray or supplicate and shed a tear everything gets solved in a minute. At the end we think, I wish I would have supplicated it a while before then everything would have been good by now . It's human nature to procrastinate to feel lazy or arrogant and thus go on acting without praying but only after a moment when everything fails and you feel tired and broke from inside that is the moment everything starts to repair. So supplicate often whether to ask minor or a major thing, supplicate more and more , do not wait till things take a worst turn, supplicate supplicate and supplicate.

only a supplication can change your past by erasing your sins, present by letting you feel peace and future by changing the destiny.

supplication needs no words, a tear and a moment of silence repairs everything. the language which can be understood only by you and your lord.

do not be impatient after supplicating, as the time of it's acceptance is from this world to hereafter so, SUPPLICATE regularly.

May Allah make us his faithful servant

Aameen

64

YOU BECOME WHAT YOU SEE

Though how many hours do we spend in our school, college or office , what matters is what we see around.

Right from the birth of a child , every development or his milestone creates a set of memories which shapes his character. A child becomes arrogant , rude, back talker, pious, righteous, good or bad according to the nature he lives in. One may deny a thousand times that what we see has no role to play with our character but a child starts to use the phone though no one taught him but all he learnt by himself only by seeing. If a mother constantly reads the Quran or any religious book automatically the child learns and tries to read too. If the father does hifdh and utters Quranic verses everyday or often , if he sees his father getting ready for prayer, applying perfume , going to the masjid ..etc he follows it unknowingly even without an effort because the parents have applied religion in their own character and the child successfully applies it too.

If the couple fights constantly , the child creates a perception of marriage as a bad thing and thus he runs away from it, if you see your mother constantly talking back to your father then you also will not stop yourself from talking back to your father. If you see your elders watching filth openly then automatically your eyes will also lose it's halal gaze even before realising that you should not watch it. You constantly go to co education places to read so, you have no realisation how these play their roles in taking you to sin and thus you fail to realise how all of the surroundings impacted you negatively but you were so busy in enjoying the forbidden acts as normal that a major haram will also have no impact on you

Though how much you deny , the reality is you become what you see.

May Allah help us to see halal, do halal and act accordingly.

Aameen

RESPONSIBILITY OF HAPPINESS

People are connected to each other through many connections but the connection you have with yourself should matter the most. Because at the end of the day or life what matters is your happiness, peace, comfort and deeds . How often we get sad because we got mistreated, abused, insulted, and criticized by others. But ask yourself who gave them the permission to disrespect you or question you , who gave them the freedom to cross the line, who gave them the authority to ruin your character or cross their boundary. No matter how close your relationship is or was nobody has to take care of your happiness or responsibility for your peace. It is yours and always belongs to yourself.

No matter how hard your day was, you deserve an appreciation from yourself to yourself because at least you survived. How many youth are giving up because they didn't lose anything but their own identity and themselves.

What you do after waking up , what you wear, what you read or what extra deed you do for the sake of Allah, what new thing you you should try that will make you happy, what time your body needs rest, what type of food you love the most, what and how much you should talk with everyone, how you allow others to treat you , where should you go that makes you happy, with whom should you go that gives you peace.... etc these are the decisions that needs no permission of other people except yourself. If the decision was right you will get rewarded and if you were wrong let alone you will bear the consequences. Thousands may advise you it is up to you to accept or reject. Because Allah has given you a capacity to think and differentiate yourself from others and if you feel so confused about being on the right or wrong path, open the Qur'an and get your guidance clearly so that the road of righteousness becomes visible. The only guts you need is to have bravery to walk on the path with a smile and act deaf to all that advice which takes you away from yourself. Our own prophet peace be upon him lost his loved ones, house, children and what not but we all know how brightened his smile was, how happy and grateful he was for his life.

May Allah help us to be happy for his sake

Aameen

LETTING BAD HAPPEN

Life is a roller coaster of happiness and sadness. We have the complete independence to feel and express both of the emotions. when we are happy every one around us start to involve in our happiness and enquires about it, and when we are sad nobody cares and seems to be uninterested in our problems.

How often we notice that when we complain of our problems or difficulties to any of our loved ones there are always a list of expected answers like *"everybody goes through it, we also faced them when we were of your age, there is no need to get sad over it, don't be a loser by crying over it, well it's your problem you must learn to deal over it, depression didn't existed during our time, these are all just baseless reasons for not being active ..etc"* .All these sentences are not positive nor helpful. Our society expects us to express happiness openly and when we are sad we should also act happy without letting anyone know about our problems and this is the blind following which has taken the lives of many youth today which prohibits the expression of sadness and frown to anyone.

There are also people who are waiting for tit for tat like our parents being strict because their parents were also strict, spouses torturing each other because they are raised in an abusive house, parents taunting/cursing/abusing/insulting their kids infornt of everyone because they think it is fine as they also went through it. The story could have have taken a positive turn if they have thought they are putting others in the same helpless situation in which they were once. Most probably the rudest people are the one who were once hurt badly but instead of not hurting others when they are given a chance they use it fully to an extent to hurt others . when they are complained about it they say "even we faced this what is the big deal?". Everybody is justifying their evil acts because once they fell into the hands of evil without thinking that it is the same pain they are giving to others. They expected help from others when they were hurt and when others ask them the help for the hurt they turn deaf. This is the cruelest rule of society which believes in tit for tat even if it means to kill someone mentally and his urge to live. Even if someone dies because of their mental harassment they would take no longer time to justify it as labelling the dead one as weak person. These are the people who never think of themselves as faulty ones instead they expect others to behave normal to their every abusive behaviour. These are the people who creates mountains of problems in others life just because they faced a problem equal to a stone in their age. The most innocent thing to think about is the one whom they hurt had no role initially in hurting them , like parents abusing their kids because once they were abused by their parents but their kids are not at fault because they didn't existed during their times nor did they hurt them but they felt prey to it. How can you justify killing someone's dreams who did not have any role in killing your dreams. This sequence goes on until a generation dies of depression.our prophet peace be upon him, never had a mindset of tit for tat instead it had a concept of forgive and move on and let

Allah handle all the matter. If we go on taking revenge then we are the one whose life will be destroyed first. So learn to forgive and move on. When you have a chance to take revenge then forgive because the more you carry the urge to hurt others the more time will be wasted. Instead cry in your prayer and move on for the people who hurted you aren't worth of your time and feelings.

May Allah protect us from hurting others.

Aameen

MIRROR OF RELIGION

We live in a world of different religions and people around you judge your religion based upon your manners and character. Though how much you may deny but that is the reality, every religion has different festivals but what makes you different should be the acceptance of your religion into your character. Religion is not limited to your clothing, hair style, festivals or food. our religion is noticed in every aspect of your character, behaviour, moral values, attitude and thinking. The religion is noticed in your every move whether you accept it's teaching or not, whether you love and respect your religion or not.

It is extremely shameful to notice that our youth are not interested in their own religion today , they ask about the existence of God openly with the intention to humiliate their own religion, but the actual reality is they hardly tried to open the book of religion even once they attempted to understand and follow it.

There are some youth who open their mind to read once a year in Ramadan only because the parents force. Our youth have miserably failed to instill love towards religion in their own heart then how can we expect to instill the teaching of religion in our society.

Our youth are busy in gaining the knowledge of world as if it is going to take them to the Jannah in the hereafter, loving the world and it's glimpses as if there is no death written, sinning openly as if there is no judgement...

During the time of our prophet peace be upon him, every youth had a different energy towards their religion, which allowed them to survive without food and gave them the strength to fight.

Today our youth has every different blessing but sadly, all these are making them arrogant and lazy.

The character they carry doesn't match even a single percent to that of the times of the prophet.

May Allah help us to read, understand and follow the religion.

Aameen

NEW GOAL EVERYDAY

Humans are special filled with emotions and it is obvious and sometimes important to get bored of your daily schedule. Hence a person switches his routine according to his personality like to travel, go on hiking or adventure , a day out, social interaction or social distance... etc. These activities not only give a break but also help the man to start fresh for the schedule or at least help him to have enough energy to survive to follow his schedule. But this is not constant as one cannot give the guaranteed intrest they may develop while handling chores an extra pressure can create chaos and one starts to lose motivation and thus slips into depression.

A person always feels happy if he is able to complete atleast a task a day, so that he feels good and proud about himself that at least there was a goal either big or small he completed it. He feels satisfied by himself. He may feel energetic to complete another task after completing a single task. Our prophet peace be upon him, often did extra good deeds but different ones to keep him going on to the right path, these are the acts apart from the obligatory acts like feeding, travelling, sitting with companions in masjid, walking with spouse, helping in house hold chores, giving charity, spending time with kids ..etc. there are numerous acts which you can do to freshen up your faith.

The only rule is that the goal should be of Religion like start to pray voluntarily, visiting an orphanage or old age, making new friends in masjid, learning a New verse from Qur'an, helping the kids to learn the Qur'an, cleaning the masjid, planting trees, reading a hadith or new islamic book, cleaning your own **room, helping your family in household chores....etc. while setting a goal remember**

The goal should be approachable.

Goal is the goal even if it is to pick up a stick or stone from the footpath.

The goal should revolve strictly around your faith.

Have a list of atleast 3/5 goals, so that you can continue doing them.

Thank Allah everytime you complete a goal.

Have a goal which is different from your schedule and nourishes your talent.

These goals not only lifts up your mood but also is a good opportunity to increase your faith.

May Allah increase our faith.

Aameen

ALL YOU HAVE IS NOW

Procrastination is a quality noticed in most of the youth today because they are busy working and earning money. The day starts and ends with office work, stress and pressure to complete the work which results in heart diseases at a young age.

There are few old people who are satisfied with the achievements they achieved during their whole life, while there are some old people who are often complaining and feeling guilty for they lost the time where they could have achieved something in their life. They spend their whole life in responsibilities, family, friends...etc and thus till the time they reach the end stage of life they find themselves alone with the thinking that it is too late to start over again. They cry and sob till the death that they couldn't do anything while reading these lines we all get a picture of someone older we know who is still complaining. But we fail to imagine ourselves in their place because we are feeling that we are living our life to the fullest but it is very obvious that you will also feel the same as they are feeling now.

All the reasons for this is constantly failing to realise that we all have an opportunity everyday and every second to change but we still waste it by complaining about the lost opportunities.

If you really need to change and achieve something then

you need to work on yourself and time schedule even if it means to spend five minutes with yourself. Our prophet peace be upon him never procrastinated when it came to religion he spread the words of peace either by action or words and to everyone either it was an old man or a young adult or a small child. So, change yourself now and save your future of hereafter as Allah loves the worship of young ones because he knows this is the age where our energy and motivation to do something is at the highest and procrastination is also at the same level. While there is also a huge chance for the youth to get distracted easily and get into the trap of the world . So, beware of your lifestyle and check on it repeatedly so that you don't lose your connection with your creator. Remember the more hard it is in the World, huge will be the reward of hereafter.

May Allah help us to change ourselves..

aameen

CHANGE YOUR PRESENT

The world is filled with people who love to see their future getting better but only one third of the people work in the present for it. Some love to get their work on time in a particular sequence, some love to procrastinate till the last minute and some love to complete the work without following any order or sequence. But everybody works but the amount of time differs from each other.

It takes a lot of strength to work in the present when you are unsure about the result in the future and for how long you need to work. The matter is not about the worldly degree of education, profession or any fame. It is about the hereafter and the matter of your religion.

Our prophet peace be upon him spread the message of peace alone, nobody imagined the amount of time and struggle it would take to spread the religion. But the people joined eventually, there are also some incidents where everyone lost hope because they lost food, house, children and friends during war , they even indulged in the war with an expectation of losing it yet it was Allah who had everything planned for the future which was bigger than anyone's imagination.

Imagine yourself working for the same thing day and night with the fear of getting killed or losing your own family but yet waking up everyday bearing every mental and physical torture yet remaining strong with the hope of everything getting well one day is the sign of a righteous believer. Each one of the companions had a different struggle but what was common was the faith which connected them with love and hope. When everything was lost they trusted allah.so,

Trust Allah when you feel lost

Trust Allah when you know you are right but everybody betrays you

Trust Allah when everyone who loved you once now hates you

Trust Allah when you are unaware of how long you will have to fight

Trust Allah when you are unsure of going wrong or right

Trust Allah everyday and every second.

When you concentrate closely then you will notice that you are already taking small footsteps towards your bigger goal unknowingly and when you reach your goal you will realise that Allah helped you in every aspect. So be grateful and patient till you reach your goal.

May Allah help us to change our present for a better future.

Aameen ❤

NEVER TOO LATE TO START

Everything has an end even to your life in this world. The hectic schedule of the day is put to an end by the night for rest and the following day is the chance for you to start all over again.

The gap of time between each prayer is to concentrate upon your faith and develop it in your actions and correct your mistakes all over again by starting the prayer with more concentration.

How will you know that it's the right time to start again...or what time is the right time to change or to start something new?

The answer to this is NOW,

You waking up healthy from bed is a chance for you to start again something positively. Your love towards prayer, waking up at the middle of the night to pray, a constant positive change in your behaviour , you are alive, breathing and healthy are the biggest signs to make you realise that it is not late yet.

If you really need Jannah don't find excuses that supports your laziness, you have a chance every minute and second to do something for yourself. Stop blaming the time, schedule, responsibility, lifestyle as reasons for your procrastination. Nobody gets a chance to start over, you need to take the risk on your own by sacrificing your worldly desires. Stop giving reasons that you couldn't pray because of a movie/tv, or you can't fast because your body gets weak or you can't read Qur'an because you don't know arabic or tajweed or you can't follow Qur'an because society is very modern ..all these reasons need to get a reality check that you can't get Jannah by doing the acts of hell.

So start , take the risk, sacrifice your desires to taste the sweetness of real faith.

May Allah bless us to start our life with positivity.

Aameen

RELIGION OF CONVENIENCE

If you had a chance to rate your lifestyle according to the religion the results would come up with negative points. Today, we are living a life with a switch of onn and off of religion which we use from time to time according to our comfort. The only two times when we fully follow the religion is during the festivals and difficulties. We turn towards Allah and his guidance as if we are his faithful servants during these times and when you desire something from this world , we neglect every ruling regarding it .

This is not regarding your acts of worship, it is a life apart from your masjid and circle of religious friends. The life you are living by running behind the world and it's false fantasies.

The switch of religion can be seen where the youth are eating meat without any assurance of it being halal or not in public places, woman praying with full hijab but displaying her Beauty in the functions, celebrating every innovation of Islam as if it is important than prayer, a woman who gives lectures on Quranic verses in public but allows every bid'ah in her own house, a man who gives charity regularly but fails to check his earnings as haram or halal, youth praying only during the Ramadan and while the whole year he spends time in clubs, drugs and alcohol. The man wants to have four wives but fails to fulfill any one of his responsibilities. This is the society we live in where everybody has a switch of religion according to their convenience to follow.

fear Allah because religion was revealed to live your life on it completely not according to your mood. Have strength and courage to follow religion without thinking about others .

Do not justify everything you do because Allah understands you is more than enough.

Whatever you do should be only to please Allah because at the end he is the one who will reward you.

May Allah help us to live life completely on religion.

Aameen

SAY WHAT IS RIGHT

Humans have a nature of thinking twice and this often puts them in a dilemma before correcting others. Sometimes it results positively while most of the time it has a negative impact as the response depends completely on the nature of the human. For example we think twice before correcting others because there are certain points to take into the light before doing so , like the role of they are elder to you then there is a high risk of misunderstanding but if the listener is a very good friend of yours or younger than you then the value of advice may have an impact.

But no matter what say right but in a different way. Approach by looking at the time, nature, mood and responsibility. Often the negative impact depends on the one who represents the right thing in a wrong way. Do not utter those words in a way that you don't like to be said to you. If something is wrong and it comes into your notice then approach to correct it when they are alone and use the language which they understand. If the way of communicating the right thing is wrong then it will result in a negative way. How often we stop ourselves only because the one who is wrong is our parents, elders or very close friends. We end up hurting ourselves and our level of faith by avoiding to hurt others. Remember it is duty of every muslim to say the right thing and stop the wrong thing in every possible way but while correcting the wrong things we often end up doing wrong. That is forcing others, Insulting/ humiliating/abusing others, ...etc. remember, Even if the world hates it or enjoys being wrong then say the right thing in a way which sounds good. Do not start lecturing every time and about everything. Say what is right but in a right way . If the world hates it let it be, but do not compromise with your faith, we see people often trying to correct others and if they don't value his words he also joins them in the wrong deed. Never compromise with the rules of your creator because of his small creations because there is no obedience to anyone while being disobedient to your lord.

Say right and if they don't listen or understand leave them for the sake of Allah. Do not drag the issue nor insult them in front of others . Even if the world hates to listen advice them till you can but at the end you have to leave them because you can't risk your faith for the worldly love. Most importantly do not hate the one who is wrong he is Just dealing with the Whispers of Satan in a different way. Pray for his guidance and leave, leave, leave them . This doesn't mean you should avoid or stop checking on them but instead just draw a thin line where he has got no authority to play with your faith. Even if no one wants to understand you should be strong enough by not letting your faith shake.

May Allah help us to say right, be right and follow the right.

Aameen

ENJOY BEING YOU

Enjoying yourself is the best thing you should say to to yourself daily to motivate yourself and be the way you are. This statement is not about your physical nature but instead it is about your every aspect. Life puts you in a situation where your real identity is questioned and remember that is the time where you have to prove yourself and for that the most important thing is to first believe in yourself and your ability. Enjoy being yourself because you are special and not your own sibling is like you in nature. Every set of yours is made different by Allah so accept the fact. This should not let you think that you are perfect instead you should accept that you have some flaws and some qualities to be admired too. Work on your flaws but not everything needs to be corrected. You can't be a chef, an engineer, doctor and teacher at the same time. You may have only a skill of which you need to work upon do not try to manage all at once our of peer pressure. Start your day by saying the statement aloud and be proud of yourself, do not change yourself for anyone except Allah. Do not mimic or copy or force yourself to be like others. Our prophet peace be upon him was also disliked by many non believers but he never changed himself for even a second to get appreciation or to get accepted. Be like him, for indeed he was blessed with many qualities but never was he arrogant about it , instead he accepted himself the way he was, he enjoyed and expressed himself the way he was. Do not feel shy for being the real you, if you don't like something express it freely, if you like something enjoy it freely.

Do not lose your value by changing yourself for others.

Stop complaining about your physical appearance and do not try to change it, the biggest sign of a righteous believer is being content with everything provided to him by his lord.

May Allah help us to accept ourselves and be happy with ourselves.

Aameen

PEACE WITHOUT ALLAH

Many people around us live freely skipping prayers and ignoring sunnah. These people have excessive desires and most of their life is spent in fulfilling these wishes. And these are the people who have every blessing from wealth to health but these are the people who are excessively arrogant. While, the righteous one who is a firm believer of Allah often feels worry or restless even if he is a minute late to his daily prayer. The righteous one is satisfied in little and concentrates more upon living the life according to the sunnah.

Everyone gets into a State of life where when the atmosphere changes we get to adjust in it like most of the youth today leave their home for worldly education they may have been raised in a religious atmosphere but as soon as they leave the home they leave their faith in no time and this happens with the time, they repent and repeat the sins only because the ability to resist the Desire becomes less and the continuous force of unreligious friends take him away from religion and his heart doesn't remind nor does his mind asks him to repent.

So, worry if you are enjoying life without religion, worry if you have health and yet you are unfaithful, disobedient, arrogant, not making supplication yet your every dua is fulfilled,... etc

Worry if you haven't taken a single step towards religion, worry if your heart hurts no more while leaving the prayer, worry if your mind doesn't remember Allah, worry if your only worry is towards this world and worry if your every work of this world is taking you away from Jannah, worry if your only concern is to fulfill your worthless desire, worry if you want to get successful in this world without caring about the halal earning, worry if your heart is calm by listening to music and restless while listening to the Qur'an, worry if your day is going fine without praying.... etc.

To stop worrying you need to start something and the best thing to break the walk of worry is repentance because unknowingly our repeated sins make our heart hard. So, repent and break the wall and let your heart experience peace by following the religion. The starting road may be full of hurdles, mainly your friends who influenced you once will turn away from you, mock and insult you and leave no stone unturned to drag you towards them. Be careful, be cautious and be aware because your own parents will be unknown to you on judgement day while your friends are the most distant ones.

May Allah allow our hearts to find peace in our prayer.

Aameen

DO NOT LOSE YOURSELF

Copying is often misunderstood as following what everyone does or what you like by following others. This includes the way of talking, using your abilities, talent and accepting yourself for who you are not or forcing yourself to change only to get accepted by society. The most common example is the killing of dreams or goals of children because they are forced by the parents to do what they are not capable of doing or they don't want to do it. This leads to a mental struggle in the mind of the acceptor, one thinks he is worthless and often many end up giving up the dreams of themselves and their parents by killing themselves. Do not lose your uniqueness because everybody is unique just like the fingerprints, there was and there will be no one like you, your talking nature, smiling, character, attitude, morals, talent... etc. Everything is unique because you are built like this. We often end up agreeing to something that we don't like only to stop or end the pressure and thereby we struggle to face ourselves because we cheat the most precious person that is ourselves. We may gain others love but we start to lose everything bit by bit and there comes a time that we lose them for whom we changed ourselves once and we find ourselves in such a state that everything is dispersed and too late to recover and cure and set up right because it would be too late. We explode our feelings in a way that it affects us for the whole life leaving us in regret and guilt. Ask your own parents, we often find them complaining that there were not enough chances for their talent to grow and nor was it allowed to showcase it, all they did was to follow their mother at home and follow the business during the youth stage which continues till the death . Even on the bed of death the only thing that makes them worry is the property and business and unfortunately not the happiness of their own children.

Our prophet peace be upon him was unique from every other prophet. His own companions had very different talents like fighting of Umar , soothing voice of Bilal, decision taking capacity of Abu bakkar...etc. these all prove that everybody is born and built differently. So do not lose yourself by forcing yourself to change for the society only to get accepted. Remember everything will fall back on its place when it's the right time. Because even our prophet wasn't accepted by society because the road he chose wasn't allowed during those times but that doesn't mean he was wrong. Every change needs time so, be strong in order to find out your talent and use it in a way that would benefit your faith to reach a higher level of paradise.

May Allah help us to use our uniqueness in a positive way.

Aameen

PRAYER OF HEART

How many times we have an instinct from our creator who gives us his signs which we clearly feel in our heart but we often fail to trust. Think carefully how often we felt an urge to pray or at least supplicate either before going out on a trip,or a job, or accepting a deal, going out with a friend, hurting someone, taking a major decision, before going to a Certain place we feel uneasy as our faith is not allowing us to move through it and when we fail to value those instincts one or the other bad things happen and later we say "i was feeling as if it was not good ..etc". Our heart is the biggest source of guidance and misguidance of our faith, if you trust it consciously by feeding it with religious knowledge it will guide you and if you feed it by satisfying it's every worldly desire it will misguide you.

Pray pray and pray especially if your heart is asking for it, how many times we feel that urge to pray no matter where we are all of a sudden we feel that " o Allah I need your help ". Accept the fact and trust your heart after all it's just a matter of minutes to pray, and how peace, comfort your heart feels after praying even if you haven't made your prayer special by supplication or crying. Yet, you feel calm as if everything will be alright from here how amazing is the feeling which you are feeling while reading this because we all have prayed like this once. We prayed once without knowing how much we needed it. Praying consciously after reaching a breaking point or getting hurt is different and praying without knowing what we are praying for and what we should ask for is completely different and both the emotions hit us in a different way and energy but takes a positive turn. So whenever you feel an urge to pray , no matter how happy or sad, or which place are you in, what time or state is it, pray pray and pray not because you need it only because Allah wants you to pray for indeed you are special because Allah called you from your heart and not from azaan. You are blessed indeed so be thankful for it. Be grateful and feel your religion in a most special way.

May Allah bless us and accept our prayers

Aameen

RESTLESS SINS

Everyone has their own personal life apart from their social life and the way they behave socially often leaves us confused. Society today is filled with people living their richest life while they are openly committing sins and we get depressed by thinking that we are fighting for our basic needs by following every rule of religion.

But at the end you see those sinful people often leave this world in a very dreadful way either by narcotics, drugs, murder, suicide....etc.

Be thankful that atleast we are alive in a healthy state of faith that is as soon as we commit a sin intentionally or unintentionally we feel sad and the sadness goes away only when we repent. Be thankful that atleast you value your religion because today we find most of the influencers are muslims but sadly the only thing that connects them to our religion is their name.

Do not feel sad When you see them going on a vacation, buying luxurious cars, going to clubs, mixed Gatherings, ...etc. only Allah knows what sins they are committing behind the cameras.

If something is making you feel restless then first be thankful that at least your faith is not dead and secondly repent and repent. Even if you are unaware of your sin, if you don't know who has been hurt, if it was a mistake or known committed intentional sin of desire...etc. make it a daily habit to say Astagfaar. Our prophet peace be upon him who hardly made a mistake also repented often. Remember, feeling sad or restless after committing sin is indeed a sign of a righteous believer. What decides your destination is what you do after feeling depressed either you repent or you allow the Whispers of Satan to enter your heart.

Satan is often successful in his evil plans during the bad Times of believer, he makes you believe that you are unworthy to repent or to get paradise, making you feel your sins are bigger than your creator's mercy, your only destination is hell so let's enjoy sins till you are alive...etc . Do not let these sins deprive you from the mercy of Allah. Whenever you feel restless then

PRAY voluntary prayer

Make supplication

Repent often and regularly

Be grateful by listing out the blessings

Do any good deed small or big

Read Qur'an...etc.

May Allah make us his servant who repents often

Aameen

BEST FORM OF LOVE

Our prophet peace be upon him, treated everyone with respect regardless of the status , age, class, profession...etc . There are many more Stories where we heard of helping the traveller, an old lady despite getting insulted helped them. **The purest form of love is to respect**which can turn the strongest enemy into a sweetest friend.

Sadly, we see our parents abusing each other during fights, so we as kids think that to insult, criticize , abuse or disrespect someone is fine when you are angry. Remember, though how long you may be together or how strong your bond was, a disrespectful word is enough to break everything. That is why, when you are angry be silent, be silent and be silent.

This is also not acceptable in any form that you allow others to disrespect your loved ones. We often see when our siblings, parents, spouses are getting disrespected we stand at the corner as if we have no role to play . We stand silent without raising our voice. Whereas if someone raises their voice to us , we are the first one to raise our hand in response to our own disrespect. This is not acceptable, the moment you choose others to treat your loved ones in any manner they can, is the moment you fail your role. Nothing, makes it fine or acceptable, asking sorry later, or trying to make it up later still may leave a spot in their heart which may take time to heal or may take it forever.

So, learn to take a stand for others like you take for yourself.

Remember, disrespecting someone is never justified, and asking sorry is always too late to make up things.

Disrespecting others and expecting from others to respect you is like stealing and wanting a reward for it.

Though how many good deeds you do for Allah, there will also be a judgement about your behaviour with people. So fear Allah.

May Allah help us to respect others.

Aameen

SAILING ON A HARAM BOAT

We need to look at our daily lives and how easily we have adjusted ourselves to fit ourselves in society and accept the fact that it is ok to do haram or sins. Sadly, we are thinking that today if you want to get accepted in this world you also need to accept the sins people are committing around us. We no longer wish to correct them because of the fact that everyone is loving the sinner today , either we are tired by correcting them or we want to run away from the truth. Sadly, this is the story of every household today , the one who stands against blindfollowing and sins is the person who is labelled as the person who is overly religious. When such a person commits even a small mistake everybody lifts their finger as if he has committed a sin and they taunt him as "look at yourself before commenting on others" . This is the world we live in, where the one who is correcting others has a huge risk and people are always watching him and waiting for him to make a mistake to describe the minor sin as a major one and insult and abuse him.

We don't correct our loved ones because we love them as if they are our lord, we don't correct them with the fear of hurting them, we accept every sin they commit out of love, giving them the authority to break every rule of religion and taste the freedom just because you love them, this is not the real love. Every love has a boundary, the greatest love is the love of Allah who is going to judge you for your intentions, the love of Allah should be superior to every love of this worldly relations. Do not justify every haram as halal because you have no strength to stop it. Do not accept every wrongdoing happening around when everything can be corrected just by a little effort. Do not turn blind to every sin they commit out of love which is just a shoulder to your lifeless body on your day of death. You are not given the authority to label the sins as haram, it is already described in Quran, all you need to do is to read and follow and help others to follow, if one is ignorant towards Allah and his rulings then forsure he has no value to your love too. Have courage to stand against sins, you May think they are my parents or siblings or friends or family, but they are just a human who made mistakes, approach them with respect and correct them but if they remain attached or turn arrogant then leave them for verily you will not be asked about anyone's deeds except yourself.

Have strength to walk out from the place of sins to save yourself. Because this world and the relationships are temporary and the journey of hereafter is permanent think about it wisely. Your one worldly decision can ruin your result of judgement day.

May Allah help us to save ourselves from haram.

Aameen

COMPROMISING WITH RELIGION

Compromising with the religion for simple worldly gain has become so common that we think it is ok to do so.

Our prophet peace be upon him and his companions were ready to sacrifice their lives for their religion and we can't sacrifice our own desires but we have the same goal and expect ourselves to be in equal space with the companions in the Jannah. But sadly, our actions are not up to the match of our intentions.

We neglect or shorten the prayer because we have a function or a marriage to attend or shopping, we neglect prayer because everyone around are non muslims in our college or school, we pray late Because the match/film/serial was so interesting, we don't read Qur'an because we want to wait for more reward that is Ramadan, we don't give charity unless it is important, we open Qur'an when someone dies Only to know the rulings on the property share , we don't supplicate because everything is fine, we wait for the difficulties in order to run back to Allah.

When you compromise with your religion in every single way then how can you expect Allah to reward you at highest level of Jannah- The main jihad is the fight against your desires-

Fight for yourself first, fight for the place in Jannah, pray for it, supplicate for it.

Ask yourself what if you die at this moment while reading my caption, will your past deeds will lead you to Jannah or not?

We just scroll, Neglect and move on. And when we see a reel with music it ultimately comes up on our lips on first hearing , while the repeated recitation of the Qur'an barely comes in your mind. That shows the level of compromise we are doing with our religion. Most of our feed section is filled with celebrities, movies, dance, ...etc and we have only a few accounts with Quranic recitations which we barely look at. . this shows the reality of compromising.

Let us stop fooling ourselves, let us start giving importance to our religion because it is the base, pillar and result of our life.

Let us check our level of faith, let us repair our faith by not compromising and being serious with every act.

let us just pause, take a break, think consciously and start again because the last chance to change is till the last breathe of life.

May Allah help us to follow religion first in every aspect of our life .

Aameen

FEELING SORRY FOR OTHERS

We often tend to get sad when someone is committing sins especially our loved ones, friends, family..etc. even when we try hard to show them the guidance they start to hate us and this creates a negative feeling in our heart about ourselves that we are not worthy to save them from their sins.

But you notice, they barely try to seek right knowledge or when they have it they fear to follow and give up their desires because they find peace in their old sins, they show zero changes in their behaviour, they get into a fight with everyone who says they are wrong or they hate those who stop them from sins and instead they carry a character like "i am what i am, let the world adjust". But this is not how the World works, because this place is not worthy of your comfort living, rather it is a test for us. A believer may have a hard time but will eventually have a greater reward. but some people try hard to get a comfortable life in this world thereby forgetting the real aim of the hereafter.

So do not waste your time in thinking about the people, or their sins or behaviour , because your thinking is not going to change them as they don't want a change within themselves. So beware of these people because even our prophet peace be upon him could not save his uncle(abu taalib) though he was so supportive yet he didn't accept the religion till the end, prophet nuuh peace be upon him, who tried his best to save his son from the punishment of Allah but it was the son who was sure of his saviour and acted arrogantly and everyone knows the end result of the Sinners.

If you really love someone, who enjoys committing sins, **Advise them . if they don't listen , pray for them and end the matter.**

As the people who go against Allah for their desires, will for sure go against your love too . Remember, you are not going to be held accountable for what they do .

Do not feel sad for them but instead pray and move on.

May Allah help us to pray for everyone.

Aameen

THANK ALLAH

The list of blessings is never ending , right from your birth to death or in a single day there are infinite blessings which if are mentioned then all the books of this world may fall short.

Thank Allah for atleast you are alive, as the value of each breath is unimaginable, how many people lost their lives during the recent outbreak of the viral disease.

Thank Allah for atleast you have a roof of shelter, for how many people's lives were destroyed in a second due to floods or earthquakes.

Thank Allah for atleast you have a set of dress to cover your body, for how many people spend wearing the same cloth for months.

Thank Allah for atleast you have different meals in a single day, for how many people stand begging for the whole day just for a handful of rice.

Thank Allah for you are getting every blessing because somene else [parents] are working to look after you, for how many infants or toddlers are left to die because they lost their guardian.

All these blessings are not earned by you , they were given to you without asking for it, but all these should make you arrogant or a complainer who finds defects in everything.

THANK ALLAH in your prayer

THANK ALLAH in your supplication

THANK ALLAH for a drop of water and a second of breath
THANK ALLAH for everything.

READ, READ AND READ

The first thing that prophet peace be upon him did during the time of quran revealation was to read. our religion has given the most of it's importance to reading because only reading can increase the knowledge and develops a character.

reading and keeping oneself updated about the world is not important rather read about the religion and follow it because the worldly education gives you a degree of paper making you eligible to survive in this world and earn only paper which is money, and a single matchstick can ruin your degree to your hard earned money. But, the knowledge you gain about the religion in this world needs no degree of confirmation because it is Allah who decides it on the day of judgement according to your intention.

The value of reading is justified only when you apply what you read.

An uneducated man with good character is beneficial to the society rather than a educated characterless man. we see the heineous crimes are committed by mostly educated people while the most loving are the uneducated ones. the educated people learn the knowledge of money to earn and survive and uneducated people have the best character even without the capability to read and write.

This doesn't mean one must not gain knowledge but rather what you read should be followed or else it is just a waste of time.

Read regularly as reading has many benefits .

Read religious book so that you may reap it's benefits in both the worlds.

Read for the sake of Allah.

The best book to start with is the holy Quran

Read for it sharpens your brain and strenghtens your heart by making it more lovable and active.

Read during the fajr or magrib time.

Read when you are alone so, atleast you will be safe from the whispers of satan for a while.

Read to change your character from better to best.

Read because there is not a single book which asks you to be a bad human, every book has a message to know, learn, understand and follow.

May Allah help us to follow what we read

Aameen

Glossary

ALLAH :
The God of muslims

HARAM :
A set of forbidden bad deeds

QURAN :
A holy book of muslims

HALAL :
A set of good deeds mentioned in the holy book

SUPPLICATION :
Form of dua done by muslims on several occassions

TAHAJJUD:
A special voluntary prayer prayed during night or just before fajar.

SINS :
A list of bad deeds

PRAYER :
Five obligatory and other voluntary prayers of muslims.

PROPHET :

A man on whom was the holy book revealed through an angel

RELIGION :

islam

REPENT :

an act of feeling guilty for the bad sins committed and thereby asking forgiveness

JUDGEMENT :

A day which begins with the end of the world and every person is judged according to his deeds

HEREAFTER :

a permanent destination of the people which begins after one's death

List of Contributors

The other books written by the author are-

GOLDEN ADVISE OF PARENTS

HALAL LOVE STORIES

WHAT LIFE TEACHES YOU

ISLAMIC LULLABIES

ISLAMIC LIFE

UNSAID FEELINGS

You can follow the author on social media as-

Nabi_e_ummah on Instagram
Or
Charge_ur_eemaan on Instagram
Or
www.firdosetarannum@gmail.com

Notes

In the name of Allah with Whose name nothing can harm on earth or in heaven, and He is the All-Hearing, All-Knowing

O Allah, You are my Lord, there is no god but You, in You I put my trust, and You are Lord of the mighty Throne. Whatever Allah wills happens, and whatever Allah does not will does not happen. There is no power and no strength except with Allah, the Most High, the Most Great. I know that Allah has power to do all things and that Allah has encompassed all things by His knowledge. O Allah, I seek refuge with You from the evil of my own self, and the evil of every creature that You hold by its forelock. Verily my Lord is on a straight path

O Allaah, Lord of Jibreel (Gabriel), Michael and Israfeel, Creator of the heavens and the earth, Knower of the unseen and the seen, You are the Knower of the unseen and the seen, You will judge between Your slaves concerning that wherein they differ. Guide me to the truth of that wherein they differed by Your leave, for You guide whomsoever You will to the Straight Path

O Allah, help me, guide me, correct me, enable me to attain what is right and earn reward, and forgive me if I make a mistake or am deprived of an answer.

O my Lord! Open for me my chest (grant me self-confidence, contentment, and boldness); And ease my task for me; And make loose the knot (the defect) from my tongue, (i.e. remove the incorrectness from my speech), That they understand my speech

-Aameen